M000050219

"Within these pages, Joann Davis lays stepping-stones that can guide us toward happiness, successful living—and a better world for all."

—Kathryn Adams Shapiro, author of *Wisdom's Choice: Guiding Principles from the Source of Life*

"This book plucked my heartstrings with its down-home anecdotes and inspiring words of wisdom and made me smile as it reminded me of what really matters in life— family, friends, all A's in school, rainbows—at least two hundred everyday joyrides that are not things. Buy this book in bulk!"

—Albert Gaulden, author of *Signs and Wonders: Understanding the Language of God* and founder and director of the Sedona Institute

"Simple yet profound principles for achieving spiritual simplicity and avoiding the rat race of materiality."

—Ron Shapiro, coauthor of *The Power of Nice* and founder of the Shapiro Institute of Negotiations

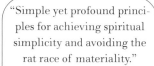

THE BEST THINGS IN LIFE
AREN'T THINGS

THE BEST THINGS IN LIFE AREN'T THINGS

AREN'T THINGS

Celebrating What Matters Most

JOANN DAVIS

BEACON PRESS *Boston*

BEACON PRESS
25 Beacon Street
Boston, Massachusetts 02108-2892
www.beacon.org

Beacon Press books
are published under the auspices of
the Unitarian Universalist Association of Congregations.

07 06 05 04 03 8 7 6 5 4 3 2 1

The Scripture quotations contained herein are from
The New Revised Standard Version Bible, copyright 1989
by the Division of Christian Education of the National Council
of the Churches of Christ in the U.S.A.

Printed in Mexico
Text design by Melodie Wertelet/mwdesign

Library of Congress Cataloging-in-Publication Data
Davis, Joann.
   The best things in life aren't things : celebrating
what matters most / Joann Davis.
      p.   cm.
ISBN 0-8070-2822-3 (alk. paper)
1. Conduct of life.   I. Title.
BJ1581.2.D3677   2003
170'.44 — dc21   2003001234

For Kenny,
who makes everything possible

Contents

Foreword

Kenneth C. Davis

"To have a reason to get up in the morning," Judith Guest began her insightful novel *Ordinary People,* "it is necessary to possess a guiding principle. A belief of some kind."

When I first read that passage back in the 1970s, it crystallized an essential truth for me: We all need words to live by. Of course, the trick is choosing the right ones. For way too long and for way too many Americans, it seems that the words have been, "Keep up with the Joneses," or "Diamonds are a girl's best friend," or "Shop till you drop."

This book suggests that you consider a different guiding principle: "The best things in life aren't things."

This is not just a clever play on the Jazz Age lyric that "the best things in life are free." These words simply distill a strain of ancient wisdom from the prophets and thinkers we supposedly revere. When I was researching my book *Don't Know Much About the Bible,* I spent hours studying the words of the Hebrew lawgivers and prophets, Jesus, Paul, and the gospel writers. I read them all. And guess what? Not even one of these inspired beings ever singled out possessing "things" as the key to satisfaction or contentment. Nor did any of the other sages of old, including the Greek philosophers, Buddha, or Confucius.

In fact, most of these enlightened ones have said exactly the opposite. "He that trusteth in his riches shall fall," Proverbs instructed. "For what is a man profited," Jesus asked, "if he shall gain the whole world, and lose his own soul?" And in China, five hundred years before Jesus was born, Lao-Tzu cautioned, "There is no calamity greater than lavish desires."

Ignoring this advice for most of its history, America has instead had a long national love affair with "things." In 1835, Alexis de Tocqueville marveled in *Democracy in America*, "I know of no country where the love of money has taken a stronger hold on the affections of men." With the twentieth century advent of mass media and merchandising, America's knack for innovation was one-upped by its genius for marketing. We had perfected the art of packaging "things" as the key to contentment, at the same time contracting a national epidemic of what has been called "Affluenza."

The empty promise of America's obsession with possessions hit home for me on September 11, 2001. Grounded on a runway in Dallas at the moment the jets hit their targets in Washington, D.C., and New York, I had only one concern in the world: How were my wife, Joann, and our two children doing at home in the West Village of Manhattan, just blocks from the World Trade Center?

Those first frantic minutes turned into hours, cut off from the "thing" that mattered most—my family. As I heard businessmen scrambling on cell phones, vainly attempting to rearrange their meetings and travel plans, I wanted to know that my family was out of harm's way. Once I knew that, I had a single desire: to get home and embrace them all. Luckily finding the last rental car in Dallas, I drove sixteen hundred miles across a changed American landscape and, two days later, was able to do that.

Back home, New Yorkers came together in ways I had never seen, and the immensity of the tragedy rolled through our neighborhood like a tsunami of loss. Our own good fortune was tempered by the news that Joann's cousin, Larry, a New York City firefighter, had been among the fallen heroes at the World Trade Center. And an old friend, Bill Biggart, a photographer who had covered danger zones like Belfast and the

Middle East, lost his life just minutes from his home and family, doing what he always did—following the firemen.

In the horrific aftermath of September 11, when we were told by our leaders to go to the mall, Joann and I knew there had to be another way. And that was the seed for this book. Its purpose is to simply declare that the time has come to shift our focus away from the obsessive pursuit of "things." In a set of simple lessons, illustrated by wisdom drawn from the world's great thinkers, this book attempts to celebrate what really makes life worth living—family, friends, fortitude, and freedom, to mention just a few. Along with our spiritual life and connections to one another, these are the simple gifts that prove what the best "things" truly are. This book's central message dares suggest that we elevate the invisible virtues and values that form our common ground and appreciate the small wonders that make life worth living. That we compose more meaningful lives through service and sacrifice.

Is this Pollyannaish or pie-in-the-sky? Or is it possible?

The book you hold says that it is not only doable but desirable. Don't buy it? Read on, and perhaps you, like us, will find yourself agreeing that "the best things in life aren't things."

THE BEST THINGS IN LIFE
AREN'T THINGS

Because the "Best Things in Life Aren't Things"

When I was in high school back in the 1960s, my ninth grade science teacher often used vivid examples of "show and tell" to get her point across. One day during a lab, for instance, while offering a lesson on evaporation, she plunged her face into a cloud of steam rising up from a pot of hot water. "The transformation of matter from one state to another requires a catalyst," she advised, pointing to a little Bunsen burner sending up a thin blue flame. We all took notes, certain these ideas would be on the quiz.

Years later, that lesson came back to me after September 11. Living in New York City, about a half a mile from the Twin Towers, I had been heading home from the dentist that morning when a group of pedestrians gathering in the middle of Hudson Street caught my attention. Approaching the crowd, I realized that every head was tilted back at an angle, craning to see the thick, black smoke billowing out of the World Trade Center just to the south. The uncharacteristic silence of this eerie scene was suddenly shattered when a construction worker with a small radio held up to his ear shouted, "And now they've hit the Pentagon!"

Seized by panic, I raced home to do the only thing that mattered—locate my husband and two teenagers. Within hours I had all of them on my radar screen, but by then the horrific enormity of the situation was beginning to emerge. Before the day was out, nearby St. Vincent's Hospital had become the unofficial headquarters of heartbreak as too few wounded had arrived for treatment, and as a wailing wall of photographs of the missing were hung on the building's facade by dazed relatives desperate for any possibility of finding their loved ones.

After weeks of funerals and memorial services, a strangeness still hung in the air. In our neighborhood, every bus stop and fire station had become a living memorial of flowers, candles, and desperate photographs of smiling people who no longer existed. Finding words to describe this surreal situation seemed futile until it dawned on me that both the city and I were experiencing a powerful catalyst. Under its influence, the world had clearly been transformed—though from what to what I wasn't really sure.

Like so many people, I felt something different going on inside of myself—in my soul—where I was eager to restore a sense of normalcy as well as learn something positive from the tragedy. In the months that followed, my husband and I talked frequently about the larger questions of life that often get lost in our day-to-day hustle to make ends meet and blindly get wherever we are going. What really mattered to us? Did we keep it in sight as much as possible and count our blessings? Trying to regain our equilibrium led us to discuss our personal priorities and how we spend our time, energy, and emotions.

One day, as we were pulling out of a parking lot near our house in Vermont, my husband, Kenny, noticed the bumper sticker on the car in front of us. "Now there are words we can live by," he said, directing me to the simple but profound inscription before us. It said, "The best things in life aren't things." Falling silent, as he sometimes does before getting to the kernel of the truth, he sighed before continuing. "Too bad it often takes tragedy to help us remember the blessings that are right in front of us."

I sat in silence for a minute, contemplating his words. Yes, I thought. It is a bit of wisdom that bears repeating—the most valuable things in life are the intangibles. Stripped of all pretense and affectation, life isn't about hard goods and services, about what we acquire and own. Life is a spiritual exercise rooted in virtue, principle, experience, spirit, faith, community, emotion, and attitude. It is a loving collaboration involving family, friends, and our dearest intimates. It is about the infinite variety and beauty of nature all around us, and the respect we must always show for the good and plenty of our world. It is about individual potential, commitment, talent, and effort. These are the most meaningful components of our life on Earth.

However, in today's consumer culture, which often associates personal well-being with our material possessions, it's easy to believe that happiness is about getting the new gold watch or SUV advertised on television. So strong is society's belief in the power of the almighty dollar to create happiness that even in the tragic aftermath of the September 11 terrorist attacks, when America was reeling from grief and pain, President Bush urged the nation to "go shopping" to regain a feeling of normalcy.

While the business of the country may be business, there is surely a better place to put our deepest aspirations than in a shopping cart. The human spirit craves something more timeless and universal. As Jesus once asked his followers, who were thirsting for true enlightenment, "What does it profit a man if he gains the world and loses his soul?"

Stopping to consider what makes life worth living—what we couldn't live without—demands an acknowledgment that beyond the financial economy there is a *spiritual economy* that needs to be recognized, valued, and nurtured. The currency in this spiritual economy isn't money or hard goods. Neither is it stocks, bonds, treasury notes, or investments. The capital in the spiritual economy is love, caring, friendship, faith, and family as well as mutual support, giving, sharing, and a real appreciation of our individual and collective gifts.

While the material economy thrives on "scoring the best deal," "cutthroat" competition, "making a killing," and "every man for himself," the spiritual economy savors the experiences that bind us together. Its focus is on lending a helping hand and being neighborly, on practicing generosity and extending forgiveness. It's about showing compassion, offering comfort to those in distress, and having the courage of our convictions. It's about being willing to stand up and take an unpopular position when the risk offers no reward except a stronger backbone.

The spiritual economy is also a piggy bank for altruism, idealism, kindness, and nobility. It's about the capacity for forgiveness and being a candle in the dark. It's about acknowledging the less fortunate and knowing that the end doesn't justify the means. It's the knowledge that everyone loses when one of us wins at all costs. It's about recognizing the gift of simple abundance and making what simplicity advocates call "a declaration of enough." It's about affection, self-sacrifice, and the honest communications that flow directly from the heart. Ultimately, it's about recognizing that people are indestructible bits of divine energy who must keep their light shining by nurturing the inner spark of goodness.

The spiritual economy is also about recognizing the profound beauty of the natural world around us. Experiencing a sunset. Rustling our feet in the multicolored leaves of autumn. Seeing a rainbow after a fresh summer rain. Noticing the infinite variety of flowers that bloom in the spring. Hearing the wind whistle on a winter's night when we are sheltered indoors by the fire. These are some of the best things in life, the things we must never lose sight of.

The little book you hold in your hands is intended to be a portable reminder of what matters most, the "things" worth cherishing. Designed to highlight some of the timeless wisdom that can help us compose a rich and meaningful life, it features a number of simple essays and a "Directory of Best Things" to help us value life's intangibles.

Before you read the words that follow, let me offer a disclaimer. I am not trained to set other people in a better direction. Nor is my life a model anybody else should consider following. Every life is full of mistakes, and I have made my fair share.

But when all is said and done, I do consider myself a warrior for optimism, as I think anybody with children must be. If something I say here applies to you, and you think you can take something valuable from it, so be it. My fervent hope is that each of us benefits from the great mist rising from the water as we experience the transformation separately and together.

Cooking Up a Recipe for a Life Worth Living

Imagine waking up one day to see a headline in the morning newspaper that reads:

BREAKTHROUGH DEVICE LETS HUMANS
HEAR WHAT OTHERS ARE THINKING

"Wow!" you exclaim. "Could such a thing be possible?" Being able to tap the minds of cheaters, liars, and "spin doctors" who think one thing but say another could deal a crippling blow to dishonesty. On the other hand, virtuous people might also be affected, since the good sometimes lie.

During World War II, for instance, when the Nazis knocked on doors and asked landlords if they were harboring Jews, Anne Frank's life was spared for nearly three years because a courageous neighbor, who had hidden the young woman in his attic, lied to the authorities. "White lies" that shelter innocent victims from hurtful realities can also constitute acts of compassion. For example, when a mom praises her little boy's "delicious" burnt toast and runny eggs, she is choosing to be kind rather than honest—and who would fault her?

The point is that intentions play a role in determining whether or not "honesty is the best policy."

But even more important than practical ethics is acknowledging that a meaningful life is the product of many essential values, honesty being just one part of the mix. Compassion, responsibility, kindness, fortitude, and courage, to name just a few important virtues, all are a part of a prizewinning formula. The secret is in learning to mix the many competing ingredients of a meaningful life in skillful proportion, never allowing one critical component to overpower another.

Now, you may be thinking, that sounds easy enough. Simply get out a mixing bowl and combine a pinch of tenderness with a dash of love, sprinkling the whole concoction liberally with courage. But try doing that when you're late for work, the clothes hamper is overflowing, the dog needs to be walked, and you feel a headache coming on. Full of trials and tribulations, life can be a difficult path to walk, fraught with hard choices and moral dilemmas. What is there to guide us as we navigate the treacherous twists and turns in the road?

Worth bearing in mind is the idea that *the best things in life are life-affirming.* Thoughts, words, deeds, and experiences that increase our personal well-being, individual potential, quality of life, and sense of fulfillment without harming another individual or group are *life-affirming.* Thoughts, words, deeds, and experiences that harm our life or the lives of others ought to be avoided or viewed as measures of last resort. The best choices we can make always support life, helping it to unfold and flourish, while bad choices cause destruction and harm, sucking away our life force and dragging everything around us down.

Since each of us is given one life to live, most of the time we are free to decide what we will do with our time and energy. Life is about making choices. Will we choose to safeguard our health, develop our gifts, enrich our community, speak and act kindly, and leave the Earth better than we found it? Or will we neglect our bodies, waste our potential, destroy the natural world, and squander the opportunities that come our way? It is each person's prerogative to decide.

Broadly speaking, the opportunities to practice "life support" fall in four basic areas. These include the choice of life-affirming words, life-affirming thoughts, life-affirming experiences, and life-affirming deeds.

Starting with words, it's important to acknowledge that we influence the world every time we open our mouths. Our manner of speaking either sends a positive or negative message out into the universe, helping to uplift those around us or to damage and harm them. Which will we choose? Will we speak life-affirming words that demonstrate respect, love, and kindness toward humanity? We will say things like, "Thank you ... I appreciate that ... I couldn't have done it without you ... and I will never forget the kindness." Or will we speak disparaging words of contempt, condescension, and aggression?

Sometimes it's scary to listen in on what has become offhand chatter at home and at work. On any given day, we might hear someone say:

"Fool—he has no clue what he is doing ..." or

"She's such an idiot. She makes that same mistake over and over again ..." or

"What a jerk. I told him not to park in my driveway. He just doesn't learn ..."

Verbal contempt has become so commonplace in everyday life that people often laugh when one person savages another with petty and disrespectful banter. Nowhere is it acknowledged that lowering the bar of civility makes it tolerable to keep lowering the bar, until we are all wallowing in the mud of incivility.

How much better would it be to honor the people around us, remembering that everyone is fighting their own hidden battles. Human nature, by all evidence, is imperfect. To err is human. And there are times when we need to act firmly to keep aggressive individuals in check. But unless we are confronted with life-threatening actions from others, it is far better to be understanding and to forgive the faults and failings we encounter. Rather than using inflammatory words to incite hostility, life-affirming words create an environment of peace, sanity, and rapport in which it is possible to achieve détente and compromise. Harsh words—though only words —penetrate the spirit, while gentle words tell the world we reject adversity, that our desire is to reduce the slings and arrows of outrageous conduct.

Perhaps it would also be wise to bear in mind the sentiments voiced recently by a minister from a small town in Vermont. Dr. James Gray of Dorset encouraged his congregation "to speak the truth in love and love the truth in each, saying strong things gently and gentle things strongly." There's a bit of wisdom in that advice of benefit to everyone.

After life-affirming words come *life-affirming deeds*. Each day, in a wide assortment of ways, each of us makes big statements about who we are through our small actions. Letting someone in a rush get ahead of us in line,

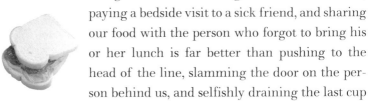 paying a bedside visit to a sick friend, and sharing our food with the person who forgot to bring his or her lunch is far better than pushing to the head of the line, slamming the door on the person behind us, and selfishly draining the last cup of coffee from the pot without regard for others. Life on Earth is about living in a community that is far happier when there is a spirit of peaceful coexistence. As John

Donne stated in his classic meditation, "No man is an island, entire of itself; every man is a piece of the continent, a part of the main." Self-centered, egotistical, and narcissistic actions that disregard the group in which we dwell are decidedly not life-affirming.

But that's only half the story. Equally damaging as crimes *benefiting* the self are crimes *against* the self. Acts of self-denial and self-neglect that impair our health and well-being must also be condemned. For instance, the failure to safeguard our bodies and get adequate rest and proper nutrition all take a toll on how we live and function. Caring for the body we have been given is a basic necessity. Mothers or fathers who carelessly neglect their own health are of no use to the children they are obligated to provide for and protect. When we ignore our own basic needs, we are greatly remiss for wasting the precious gift of life, without which we are of no use to anyone.

That's why it's important to fill each day with life-affirming actions. Regarding our personal well-being and the life of those around us as precious resources means being fair and showing mutual concern for our family, colleagues, and neighbors, never hoarding the resources that are meant to be shared or denying ourselves a life-affirming share.

A third important category that each one of us must attend to is *life-affirming experiences.* These are the oc-casions that touch our spirit and make us feel alive. Walking on the beach, getting together with an old friend, reading a good book, soaking in a hot tub, visiting a friend's newborn, going on a spiritual retreat—each of these experiences offers a natural high that make us feel genuinely alive by connecting us to the invisible whole.

The experiences that achieve these life-affirming sensations of awe and wonder may differ from person to person. Hiking to the top of a mountain may be one person's restorative while someone else may find their elixir by sitting at the opera and being transported by the sound of the human voice and orchestra. Born with the capability to experience life through our senses, each of us may find the thrill of living in a different way—through sight, touch, smell, taste, or sound. Though available in many varieties, life-affirming experiences are easy to recognize because they have something in common—they help us transcend our humanness and be connected to something infinitely larger. They expand our awareness of who we are and what life is all about. They make us feel the extra sensory thrill and awe that can carry us out of the pedestrian and everyday experiences that come from our workaday lives. We connect with ourselves and with others in profound and moving ways.

How much better is it to engage in a life-affirming, uplifting experience than to hang out on the street corner with a bored group of friends who complain about being idle? Or go to work at a job we don't like, never examining our other options? How much better is it to seek the thrill and excitement of change and possibility than it is to live a deadening existence, wasting the precious life force we are born with? For it is better to have the life-affirming experience of lighting a candle than to curse the darkness.

And finally, life-affirming thoughts are a necessary component of a meaningful and rich life. Because our thoughts and dreams are often stepping-stones to reality —the seedbed of action—it is important to maintain quality control over the ideas in our head. Thoughts of jealousy, anger, revenge, rage, aggression, and hostility can give rise to complementary action of the same nature. Instead of brooding, worrying, fretting, resenting, and being anxious, how much better to bathe our thoughts in fairness, kindness, consideration, affection, and generosity? To be constructive with our thoughts and use them as a staging area that can help to pave the way for a better tomorrow.

That way, if the day ever dawns when we wake up and see a headline that announces that someone has invented a device to tap our thoughts, our heads will be swimming with life-affirming ideas that we are proud to think. We will be living a life-affirming existence, one that demonstrates regard for ourselves and those around us. And if a threatened family comes to our door asking for shelter in our attic, we will do our very best to offer a life-affirming response. And if the authorities come knocking and ask if anyone is hiding in our attic, we will know the life-affirming response, even if it is a lie, and we will speak it in good conscience.

To affirm life or destroy it. In the final analysis, little else matters. Each one of us, in turn, must choose what we will do with our thoughts, words, and deeds. And for the rest of our lives, each of us will have to live with our choices and their consequences.

Have You Caught a Nasty Case of "Affluenza"?

Conventional wisdom tells us to "feed a cold and starve a fever." But when the patient is suffering from "affluenza," what's the best remedy?

For over fifty years, since the post–World War I economic boom spawned the "prosperity illness" dubbed "affluenza" by a PBS special, cases have been cropping up at alarming rates throughout America. Combining the "swollen expectations" of an increased standard of living with a virulent strain of "shopping sickness," affluenza is a social disease in which the drive to acquire "things" overwhelms all reason, making us a people who are only happy when we buy. Pursuing endless amounts of "stuff" makes the need to shop so essential that it feels, at times, more important than life itself.

If you want a better picture of what's been occurring, let's tour the national landscape where the "malling of America" has affected our collective lives. In the last several decades, fueled by commercial interests, the planning of our cities and suburbs has been virtually dictated by "developers" intent on attracting consumers to "shopping destinations." The resulting strip malls, enclosed malls, and the ultimate "Mall of America" offer artificial environments that attempt to satisfy every facet of our lives—from going to the dentist and clothing our bodies to buying our books and eating our meals. In the period of economic expansion that marked the 1990s, this arena of variety was more than the spice of American life. Combined with credit card excess, it was part of the fuel that made the American economy go.

And go and go and go—often into debt!

Our bloated desire to keep going takes many forms. Sometimes it appears as family discord, manifest by a need to "keep up with the Joneses." But it can also pose a threat to the environment, which suffers each time a gas-guzzling car races down the highway. Perhaps most dangerous of all, a lifestyle built on waste and excess can produce a "soul sickness" that makes happiness seem as ephemeral as yesterday's fashions, destroying one's chance for true and lasting satisfaction. The feeling that "enough is never enough" can eat away at the spirit and damage the soul.

While the "equal opportunity" plague of affluenza ravages everyone, it is especially lamentable in children. Influenced by those around them, children are clearly at risk of catching affluenza when every sentence out of their mouth begins with the words, "Can I have ..." "Will you get me ..." or "Can I get." Other telltale signs that a child may have early onset affluenza are the tendency to declare last year's model "too old" or "useless," rather than a "favorite"; to routinely demand the "super size" portion without regard for appetite; and to enjoy pushing a miniature shopping cart sporting a "Customer- in-training" flag around the supermarket.

Know the Symptoms

As the PBS show indicates, spotting a nasty case of affluenza is easier with a checklist of symptoms in hand. Here are three warning signs that may indicate you are dealing with a full-blown outbreak:

1. You frequently go shopping as a form of recreation or therapy. As a matter of fact, you think of the mall as your home away from home, a place anybody can feel good by opening their wallet.
2. You no longer try to distinguish what you want from what you need—and see absolutely no reason to bother. After all, spending money means you are doing what the President asked—supporting the economy and being patriotic.

3. You see a bumper sticker that says, "I shop therefore I am," and get an adrenaline rush.

Get Your Affluenza Shot

Rather than waiting for the symptoms of affluenza to rear their ugly head, it is far wiser to take precautions. As the old saying goes, an ounce of prevention is worth a pound of cure. So here is a three-part inoculation plan that has proven effective:

Make what proponents of the voluntary simplicity movement call a "declaration of enough." Begin examining what you consume and why you consume it. Bear

 in mind that life is made up of choices. While there are occasions when splurging is justified, overconsuming ought to be the exception to the rule. And you benefit by making a distinction between what you need and what you want. At the same time

you consider cutting back and being realistic. We all have desires and we all want to be comfortable. The need to moderate is not a call to become hermits huddling around a flickering candle flame or monks living a monastic life. Moderation is about achieving balance, both in our personal lives as well as in our culture. Enjoying beauty and feeling good in our new clothes does not mean making them our gods or the keys to our happiness.

Join the voluntary simplicity movement. For many years, idealists and activists have been scaling back their possessions, discovering that "small is beautiful," that "bigger isn't better," and that "less is truly more." Set aside a period of time to shed some things you rarely use and really don't need. Make sure your overflow goes to a worthwhile cause. And finally, count your blessings. Make it a point to consciously recognize that your true blessings transcend material objects. Appreciate the love and companionship of those around you. It doesn't cost a single dime, and provides so much.

Most important of all, don't assume that affluenza is a terminal illness.

If you attack the symptoms of this lifestyle disease early and aggressively, you will find yourself restored to the peak of spiritual health.

Don't Learn to Make a Living—
Learn to Make a Life

Becoming a doctor was a lifelong dream for twenty-one-year-old Joshua. But when the young man decided to apply to medical school, he wanted to hear what wise old Dr. Phillips, his family physician, had to say about a career in medicine.

"I could complain about HMOs adding to my paperwork," Dr. Phillips told the young man. "And I could rail about rising malpractice costs that mean scheduling more patients each day than I would like. But to nurture a newborn baby, to give comfort to a grieving widow, or be able to ease the suffering of a sick old-timer—these are the things that give meaning to my life. To a young person who feels the call to be a doctor, I say—let nothing stand in your way."

To feel the call. How seldom in today's pragmatic world—if ever—do we hear those words spoken? "Being called," for students of Bible history, is a phrase that conjures up a vision of religious converts like Paul being struck on the road to Damascus and forsaking his status as a Roman soldier to become a missionary. Nowadays, when people say they feel "called," they are usually describing their decision to enter the ministry, though more often than not they've been summoned to jury duty!

Now, let's be honest. In the modern world, where the stock market index crawls along the bottom of our television screen every night, career choice and being called have little in common. More often than not, career selection is a direct function of *salary considerations.* The defining question for many young people who leave school and enter the cold, cruel world is not what they really want to do with their lives or what they feel in their hearts is natural and best. It's about what they can *afford* to do. Seeking a job often boils down to the question: *How much does it pay?* This concern is so ingrained in our culture that high school and college counselors distribute literature on "the highest paying fields" and "job concentration surveys" that rate the best prospects.

The influence of these steering devices has proven so potent in the last few decades that college graduates in record numbers have stampeded to business school to get an MBA that guaranteed a six-figure starting salary. Getting on board the "Show Me the Money" train to Wall Street occasionally reflects a person's love of finance and money management. But more often than not, the incentives are fat paychecks, corporate perks, and retirement benefits, accompanied by a desire to become a millionaire before age thirty.

Now, again, let's be honest. Most individuals in the modern world are not financially independent or even remotely wealthy. For all intents and purposes, finding a job and working is not a choice—it is a necessity that enables the average person to pay the bills and be self-sufficient. The trouble starts to brew when money be-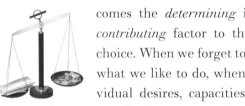comes the *determining* issue rather than a *contributing* factor to the process of career choice. When we forget to weigh and measure what we like to do, when we forget our individual desires, capacities, and limitations—when we totally ignore our *calling* and enslave ourselves to the job that pays the bills—we run the risk of focusing too much attention on *making a living* and neglect the urgent need to *make a life* built on satisfaction, passion, and meaningful work.

Take a minute and think about it. How many times have you heard somebody say one of the following things:

"I hate what I do—I can't wait to retire."

"I live for the weekends so that I can do what I really like to do."

"I like to work with my hands but instead I push paper all day."

"I work in an office—but I would rather be outside."

"This job pays the bills but if I had it to do over..."

And conversely, how rare it is to hear someone say:

"I love my job. It's such a pleasure to wake up each day and go to work."

"I wouldn't trade my job for anything else in the world."

"I'm willing to settle for a little less money because I do what I love."

The people who make the comments that fall in the first group of remarks are out of sync with the purpose of their life, while people who say things like those in the second group have discovered a critical balance between meaningful work and adequate compensation.

The question is: How can more people wind up in the second group?

The starting point for a life of meaningful work begins with an honest evaluation of what we are able to do and what we are not able to do. As Socrates once advised, it is crucial to "know thyself" in order to achieve a life of harmony and purpose. A person who is not good with his hands will probably have a hard time making a living as a carpenter, just as a color-blind woman is unlikely to succeed as a decorator, and a man who is allergic to flowers will suffer as a florist no matter how much he likes roses. Focusing on "right livelihood" means being realistic about our talents, leanings, and desires.

But self-knowledge on its own is not enough. A second major requirement for developing a life of purposeful work is to banish the idea that time is money. Ever since the dawning days of the Industrial Revolution, a view of life as an exercise in productivity has gained a dangerous stranglehold on human thinking. This faulty notion seems to have first crept in when factory owners realized that higher profits hinged on measuring the "productivity of labor" against standardized targets. For instance, if workers on the conveyor belt weren't assembling "x" widgets in "x" amount of time, money was being lost because "time equals money." Insufferable work conditions flourished as factory owners went to any lengths to cut corners to increase productivity, sometimes allowing exhausted workers and even unpaid child laborers to die on the job.

As if this this utilization of humans as cogs in the wheel of the workplace was not indecent enough, intellectual corruption also set in. A broad-scale error in thinking put machines up on a pedestal because they were faster, more consistent, and more enduring than their human counterparts. Machines didn't complain, take coffee breaks, or demand workmen's comp like those silly humans. A new age that put machine over man was dawning.

Well, maybe on the assembly line, where humans are no more than a perverse extension of the soulless machines they operate, machine efficiency is appealing. But the value of efficiency has limits. Ask keyboard operators who are afflicted in record numbers with cases of carpal tunnel syndrome because their employers demand a draconian "keystroke output" every workday. When efficiency begins to degrade life and the human soul, it needs to be put in check. Safeguarding the creative spark that resides in the human soul so that it can unfold is one of the very best things in life.

A person choosing a career is a soul unfolding. For this miraculous process to occur, it is important to see 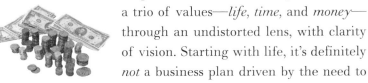 a trio of values—*life, time,* and *money*— through an undistorted lens, with clarity of vision. Starting with life, it's definitely *not* a business plan driven by the need to get the greatest return on investment. *Life* is a spiritual framework in which the intangible essence of each person—their soul—gets a chance to unfold, learn, and grow through trial, error, experience, meaningful work, pain, suffering, and joy. Neither is *money* the be-all and end-all of life but rather a means to a variety of ends. If we make money our god, as the saying goes, it will plague us like the devil. Taking care not to worship false gods of any kind is a necessity in a meaningful life. And finally, *time* is not a vehicle for making money. It is an arena in which we get to play out our hopes and dreams. These include the opportunity to do a whole host of interesting things, including the chance to follow our calling.

Which brings us back to young Joshua. On his way home from Dr. Phillips's house, the young man took a seat in the back of the bus and recalled the old family physician's inspiring words, which triggered thoughts of the great healers through the ages who undoubtedly had been "called" to serve. Albert Schweitzer setting up a clinic in Africa. Mother Teresa in India, serving the needs of the leprous children who nobody else would touch for fear of contamination. Would anything hold these individuals back from their missions?

Would Mother Teresa, for instance, have ever refused to help a patient who didn't have health insurance? Would Dr. Schweitzer consider his mission a failure because it didn't turn out to be a cash cow? Of course not. The very thought is ludicrous. Dedicated people who derive meaning and satisfaction in their work find ways to meet the obstacles in their path. Even if there are moments that seem endless and thankless, they persevere.

A Matter of Principle

"Stand by for zero hour," the military attaché called out as he read the clock on the wall of the situation room. "If we don't respond to the kidnapper's demands soon, we could be facing a bloodbath."

"Negotiating with the terrorists isn't an option," answered the security chief as he drew a handkerchief from his pocket and mopped the sweat from his brow. With a siege under way at an overseas embassy, the tension in the air was unbelievable.

"Why not do what is expedient?" argued the attaché. "Lives are at stake."

"Expediency is for the hour while principles are for the ages," said the chief, quoting from nineteenth century general and military strategist Karl von Clause-witz. "Lives may be lost today, but we will follow the course of what we believe is right."

A scene from a high-stakes military thriller? It could have been. But more than likely, this dialogue or one similar to it has played out in real life recently in some part of the world. As extremists have made it their goal to disrupt the equilibrium of free societies, one of the results has been a heightened awareness of the rules, assumptions, and truths governing free societies—their *principles*.

Principle. Take a minute, if you will, and meditate on the word. Let it filter through your mind and flood your senses. If it takes a minute to get a handle on the concept, don't be surprised. Though the word is commonly used in everyday conversation, a principle is an abstraction that can be tricky to grasp.

For many people, the concept of a "principle" will immediately conjure up some of the familiar colloquialisms we hear spoken every day—*"It's the principle that counts,"* or *"I am taking a stand on principle,"* or *"He was a man of principle."*

Historical examples of principled people may also spring to mind. One of the best known examples from American history is the patriot Patrick Henry, who secured a place in posterity by uttering the words "Give me liberty or give me death." Cherishing freedom meant Henry was willing to forfeit life rather than see his precious liberties curtailed.

Surveying writers who have weighed in on the subject can also be illuminating. While Ralph Waldo Emerson noted that "the value of a principle is the number of things it will explain," Henry Kissinger took a more ironic view, arguing that "while we should never give up our principles, we must also realize that we cannot maintain our principles unless we survive." Offering more of an overview was biographer E. M. Standing, who once observed,

A principle—as its very name implies—is something which comes first. A principle is a master key which opens a thousand locks, a compass which will guide you, even on uncharted seas.

Pinpointing the intrinsic values that can be our compass on the uncharted seas of life is a little like getting a map to ensure that we find our way to an unfamiliar destination. Without principles to help us navigate our journey through life, we may be tempted to detour through the roiling waters of expediency, which can swallow us up before we get our bearings.

Though time-consuming, the process of identifying our principles is well worth the effort because it can help to reduce indecision and uncertainty. Perhaps the process ought to begin with an investigation of the words and ideas of great thinkers who have filled books and libraries with their observations about the art of living a meaningful life. The inspirational passages provided in the following pages are intended to be the first baby steps forward in a journey of exploration designed to illuminate our personal ideology. The journey may take a lifetime, but there are untold riches awaiting those who choose to travel on the path of discovery.

A Little Directory of Principles — and Probing Questions

Individuality—*Will you be your own person or march to the beat of someone else's drum?*

As Robert Lindner so eloquently writes in *Must You Conform?*, "Adjustment—that synonym for conformity—is the theme of our swan song, the piper's tune to which we dance on the brink of the abyss, the siren's melody that destroys our senses and paralyzes our will."

And Emerson observes, "No one ever accomplished anything who did not listen to the still small voice which is his alone."

Human Potential—*Will you create a society in which every person has an opportunity to develop his or her life-affirming skills and talents?*

"Indeed, there are so many abilities in the world which fortune never bring to light," wrote clergyman Thomas Fuller in the seventeenth century.

"Let the beauty of what you love be what you do."
—Jalal al-Din Rumi, thirteenth century Persian poet

Principle—*Will you recognize the quintessential importance of valuing your ideas and ideals?*

"Action from principle, the perception and performance of the right, changes things and relations; it is essentially revolutionary; and does not consist wholly with anything which was. It not only divides states and churches; it divides families; ay, it divides the *individual,* separating the diabolical in him from the divine."
—Henry David Thoreau in "Civil Disobedience"

Morality—*Will you be flexible or rigid in applying a code to human conduct?*

"The way to avoid evil is not by maiming our pas-

sions but by compelling them to yield their vigor to our moral nature. Then they become, as in the ancient fable, the harnessed steeds which bear the chariots the sun."
—Henry Beecher Ward in *Life Thoughts*

Duty—*Will you join in the contest of life and do your duty or sit on the sidelines?*

"For us is the life of action, of strenuous performance of duty; let us live in the harness, striving mightily; let us rather run the risk of wearing out than rusting out." —Theodore Roosevelt in his speech "Duties of a Great Nation"

Self-Actualization—*Will you act in accordance with what you think and believe?*

"No being can be what he is unless he is putting his essence into action in his field." —Arnold Toynbee in *A Study of History*

"What we think, we become." —Buddha

Wisdom—*Will you understand that not doing is often-times the same as doing?*

"He who sees the inaction that is action and the action that is in inaction, is wise indeed." —*Bhagavad Gita*

The Common Good—*Will you see your deeds as often having an impact on the larger group in which you dwell?*

"Let every action aim solely at the common good." —Marcus Aurelius

Modesty—*Will you seek recognition or be content unto yourself?*

"Well done is better than well said." —Benjamin Franklin

Consistent Behavior vs. Hypocrisy—*Will you practice what you preach?*

"I have always had a horror of words that are not translated into deeds, of speech that does not result in action—in other words, I believe in realizable ideals and in realizing them, in preaching what can be practiced and then in practicing it." —Theodore Roosevelt

Quality of Life—*Will you measure success by what you have or how you live?*

"To live content with small means; to seek elegance rather than luxury, and refinement rather than fashion; to be worthy, not respectable, and wealthy, not rich; to listen to stars and birds, babes and sages, with open heart; to study hard; to think quietly, act frankly, talk gently, await occasions, hurry never; in a word, to let the spiritual, unbidden and unconscious, grow up through the common—this is my symphony." —William Henry Channing, nineteenth century clergyman, reformer

Balance and Harmony—*Will you avoid the plague of "conspicuous industriousness" and value people for who they are rather than what they do for you?*

"Nowadays, people don't ask how you are, they say, 'Are you busy?' Conspicuous industriousness is the rule." —Richard Stengel in *The New Yorker*

"The superficiality of the American is the result of his hustling. It needs leisure to think things out; it needs leisure to mature. People in a hurry cannot think, cannot grow." —Eric Hoffer in *The Passionate State of Mind*

"There is nothing, not even crime, more opposed to poetry, to philosophy, to life itself, than this incessant business." —Thoreau in his essay "Life Without Principle"

The Willingness to Engage—*Will you dare to join the contest of life or will you choose to stand on the sidelines?*

"It is not the critic who counts, not the man who points out how the strong man stumbles or where the doer of deeds could have done them better. The credit belongs to the man who is actually in the arena, whose face is marred by sweat and dust and blood, who strives valiantly, who errs and comes short again and again … who knows great enthusiasms, the great devotions, who spends himself in a worthy cause … and who, if he fails at least fails while daring greatly, so that his place shall never be with those cold and timid souls who know neither victory nor defeat." —Theodore Roosevelt

By Any Means Necessary?—*Will the perceived importance of your mission override all rules and principles, and allow you to stoop to terrorist acts that harm innocent civilians?*

"Our objective is complete freedom, complete justice, complete equality, by any means necessary." —Malcolm X in *Malcolm X Speaks*

Service—*Will you continue to share your gifts as long as you possibly can?*

"It is nonsense for you to talk of old age so long as you outrun young men in the race for service and in the midst of anxious times fill rooms with your laughter and inspire youth with hope when they are on the brink of despair." —Mohandas K. Gandhi in *The Diary of Magadev Desai*

"The best way to find yourself is to lose yourself in the service of others." —Gandhi

Liberty in Balance—*Will you honor and defend it?*

"The love of liberty is the love of others. The love of power is the love of ourselves." —William Hazlitt, nineteenth century English essayist

"Those who would give up essential liberty to purchase a little temporary safety deserve neither liberty nor safety." —Benjamin Franklin

Personal Courage—*Will you reach inside and find the strength to face society's wrath when you believe that your course is right and just?*

"Few are willing to brave the disapproval of their

fellows, the censure of their colleagues, the wrath of their society. Moral courage is a rarer commodity than bravery in battle or great intelligence, yet it is the one essential vital quality for those who seek to change a world that yields most painfully to change." —Robert F. Kennedy

Personal Ambition—*Will your personal wants and desires carry you away?*

"All ambitions are lawful except those which climb upwards on the miseries or credulities of mankind." —Joseph Conrad

The Power of Money—*Will your principles and privileges be for sale?*

"My point is that anybody that wants to be an ambassador wants to pay at least $250,000." —Richard M. Nixon on the notorious Watergate tapes

Moral Courage—*Will you speak out when the cause is unpopular?*

"A thousand men will march out the mouth of a cannon where one man will dare spouse an unpopular cause." —Clarence Darrow

Valuing Justice—*Would you take up arms to defend it for one and all?*

"Justice is indiscriminately due to all, without regard to numbers, wealth, or rank." —Supreme Court justice John Jay

Experiencing Good and Evil—*Will you turn a blind eye of indifference when something appears wrong?*

"The true evil is not the weakening of the body, but the indifference of the soul." —Andre Maurois in *The Art of Living*

Evasion—*Will you cop out on life, as if living were an exercise in duck and cover?*

"There's a scheme of evasion that has gotten into everybody. It's as though people were to say, 'I get home dog tired after a terrible day out in that jungle, and then I don't want to think about it. Enough! I want to be brainwashed. I'm going to have my dinner and drink some beer, and I'm going to sit watching TV until I pass out—because that's how I feel.' That means people are not putting up a struggle for the human part of themselves." —Saul Bellow in "Matters Have Gotten Out of Hand" in *U.S. News and World Report*

Will you struggle to preserve the human part of yourself, making it a point to define and defend who you are? Will you collaborate or be a maverick? Share or hoard? Cherish peace or instigate conflict? Will you seek truth or routinely engage in deceit? Will you honor life, liberty, and the pursuit of happiness? Or will you approach zero hour with a desire to settle for the rough and expedient ways of the world in which the end justified the means, that hits first and hits hard, that takes no prisoners? On the journey that is life, each in turn must decide.

"If I speak in the tongues
of mortals and of angels but
do not have love . . ."

When *Love Story* became a huge best-selling book and box office hit back in the early 1970s, one line of dialogue from the screenplay by Erich Segal captured headlines around the world. As brief as it was simple, it went like this:

> Love means never having to say you're sorry.

While some considered the line a profound universal truth expressed in poetic shorthand, others dismissed it as sentimental drivel for the tearjerker set. Whichever side of the debate you were on, one thing was certain—the tagline helped lift the movie and book to the number one spot in virtually every market in the world.

Well, thirty years have passed, and the debate remains unsettled. Does love mean "never having to say you're sorry"? Even now, it depends on who you ask. Advocates of unconditional love say remorse and guilt have no place in a loving relationship. Apologies are unnecessary, this faction says, because love needs no explanations. Meanwhile, those who extol the cleansing and renewing power of forgiveness are convinced of the worth of acts of contrition. They welcome the powerful tonic of a soul-baring confession to get a shaky relationship back on track.

While the jury may remain divided, one thing is certain. Love is a subject of abiding fascination. Take a look around and you will see that love is not just the stuff of romance novels and movies. It is a dominant and enduring theme of poetry, cartoons, comic books, music, television programming, and stage dramas. Not only do we have a designated holiday honoring love— Valentine's Day—there are greeting card stores in every town brimming over with love-affirming messages. Love is one of the most written about, talked about, and cried over subjects, and has been since ancient times, when the author of the Song of Solomon wrote: "Eat, friends, drink, and be drunk with love."

That's right. Even going back to one of the earliest written testaments in existence—the Bible—love is a predominant theme. The Old and New Testaments are so full of talk of love that the references are too numerous to count. And down through the ages, the theme endures. From Solomon and Sappho through Shakespeare and Elizabeth Barrett Browning, right on through to the songs of the Beatles, love may be the longest-running thread in the story of humankind.

The reason is obvious. Love is undeniably one of the *best things in life.* After the precious gift of life itself, love is arguably the greatest gift of all because it connects human beings to one another through a bridge of caring, intimacy, and affection. These spiritual nutrients are not the deserts of human experience—they are its main course. Without them, humankind would starve, wither, and die in a collective "failure to thrive."

Nor is love the province of romance. As Browning noted, love is manifest in so many varieties that we must "count the ways." The protective love of the mother and father for the newborn. The platonic love of one friend for another. The "brotherly" love of one sibling for another. The mystical love of soul mates who feel their love has connected them for all eternity— the gifts of love are manifest in as many delicious versions as there are flavors of Ben and Jerry's ice cream. Though different in nature, the varieties of love are similar in essence. All are life-giving and life-affirming. All bear the hallmarks so beautifully expressed in 1 Corinthians 13, one the most classic and far-reaching pieces of literature ever to have been recorded. There it is written:

If I speak in the tongues of mortals and of angels, but do not have love, I am a noisy gong or a clanging cymbal. And if I have prophetic powers, and understand all mysteries and all knowledge, and I have all faith so as to remove mountains but do not have love, I am nothing. If I give away all my possessions and if I hand over my body so that I may boast, but do not have love, I gain nothing.

Love is patient, love is kind. Love is not envious or boastful or arrogant or rude. It does not insist on its own way. It is not irritable or resentful. It does not rejoice in wrongdoing but rejoices in the truth. It hears all things, believes all things, hopes all things, endures all things.

Love never ends. But as for prophecies, they will come to an end; as for tongues they will cease, as for knowledge it will come to an end. For we know only in part and we prophesy only in part, but when the complete comes, the partial will come to an end. When I was a child, I spoke like a child, I thought like a child, I reasoned like a child, when I became an adult, I put an end to childish ways. For now we see in a mirror dimly, but then we will see face to face. Now I know only in part, then I will know fully even as I have been fully known. And now faith, hope and love abide, these three. And the greatest of these is love.

Little can be added to Paul's insightful appraisal, except to wonder where the prophet may have stood on the question posed by Erich Segal. Does the mystical power of love—so gentle and kind—mean never having to say we are sorry? Each of us can only hope to find the answer for ourselves one day in a relationship so warm, protective, and enduring that the answer will be apparent.

To Serve, to Lead,
and to Change the World—
through "Soul Intensity"

Congresswoman Shirley Chisholm once said, "Service is the rent we must pay for room on this Earth." How wonderful life would be if everyone agreed with Chisholm—and wrote a check on the first of every month for their "planetary room and board." With service contributions to the poor and the needy flowing in steadily, Earth would be a place of greater kindness, generosity, and equality.

But life on Earth isn't like that. While some members of humanity do more than their share to serve the needs of humankind, many others do little or nothing. An ever-widening division between the haves and have-nots has made Earth a dog-eat-dog world based on the survival of the economically fittest. Of course there are charities and relief funds that help the poor, as well as volunteer organizations designed to assist the homeless, the hungry, and the disadvantaged. Exceptional individuals like Mother Teresa and Desmond Tutu have even devoted their lives to good works and acts of mercy. But by and large, these people and their efforts are exceptions to the rule.

It's time to change all of that. But how do we do it? Perhaps, as with every great fire, it must begin with a tiny spark. Great undertakings often begin with a simple idea germinating in the heart of a dedicated individual. As Thomas Carlyle once said, "Great actions are sometimes historically barren while the smallest actions have taken root in the moral soil and grown like banana forests to cover whole quarters of the world." The eminent writer Samuel Taylor Coleridge added his two cents to the argument when he wrote that "all the great—the permanently great—

things that have been achieved in the world have been so achieved by individuals working from the instinct of genius or of goodness."

Working from an impulse of goodness to improve the lot of the downtrodden does not mean forging ahead with Pollyannaish expectations. Let's be realistic. The world didn't get this way overnight. Widespread and lasting change will take some time. But as we look around our planet we can take heart from the momentous political and social shifts that have taken place in our lifetime, ushering in real changes that have had an impact on quality of life both at home and abroad. Not only has the Berlin Wall come down in Germany and the Soviet Empire dissolved into dozens of fragments, there is now a ban in many public places in America on lighting up a cigarette. Smoking, once a fashion statement and status behavior, became "the cooties of the twentieth century," in the words of one editorial writer who noted how shivering employees huddled in the doorways of great office buildings in inclement weather because they were prohibited from polluting the air breathed in by their coworkers.

Without any question, progress is being made. So, no matter how bleak the outlook, let's not be pessimistic about our ability to improve the world. When there is a strong belief system in place, the possibility exists for a tremendous surge of momentum capable of bringing about profound, sweeping, and long-lasting shifts. The key is in finding and tapping into a reservoir of energy that can sustain us on our quest. As the American philosopher Eric Hoffer once noted, "Momentous achievements are rarely the result of a clean forward thrust but rather of a *soul intensity* generated in front of an apparently insurmountable obstacle that bars our way to our cherished goal."

Soul intensity. Now there's a seldom-mentioned but valuable commodity. Like a precious store of gold bullion, soul intensity is money in the vault waiting to earn greater interest by being more wisely invested. Attracting our eye with its singular luster, soul intensity is an extraordinary asset to any who put it to use. It is the spark plug in the engine. The source of ignition that can propel the enterprise forward. The fire in the belly of the motivated.

Though it isn't advertised for sale in the newspaper, and you won't find it stacked up on skids at the price clubs, there is good news to report about soul intensity. It exists within each and every one of us. We were born with it. It is our birthright. Like the proverbial light being kept hidden under the bushel, soul intensity is a great potential waiting to be turned on to help illuminate a dark place.

Switching it on is really quite easy. It begins with the simple acknowledgment that we desire a better world. Too much time is spent talking our problems to death. Corrective action sometimes gets buried under profuse verbiage. We talk the problem to death but never do anything about it. Let us begin with a basic acceptance of the fact that the world is an unfair place and that it is our intention to *be the change* we want to see implemented. Then, let's cut the talk and move on. Perhaps it is wise to take a page from the book of the late political activist Abbie Hoffman, who once advised his radical followers, "Never explain what you are doing. This wastes a good deal of time and never gets through. Show them through your actions."

Once your willingness to act is strong, be prepared to jump in. It has been said that the Red Sea only parted after the first Jew plunged into the water. Jumping in can take a lot of forms. But it only has to take one form, which can be very personal to you. If you are targeting the problem of social inequity, stop in at the local high school tonight and volunteer to tutor one evening a week. After you eat your next Thanksgiving dinner, go to the homeless shelter in your town and offer to ladle out the mashed potatoes. Tutoring a prisoner to read and write may be your calling if you love English—so pick up the phone and make a call to find out how you can make it happen. Each individual must determine his or her own course.

"With me," George Washington once said, "it has always been a maxim to let my designs appear from my works rather than from my expressions." So there it is stated so clearly: *Let your designs appear from your works.*

Another avenue for change comes from accepting the idea that service is a first cousin of leadership. All those who hold any platform of responsibility within a group—be it a company, a family, a corporation, an organization—can effect the greatest change by viewing themselves as the humble servants of their charges. The old-school management style of "top down" delegation offers little incentive for the people at the bottom of the hierarchy to respect the people at the top, save for fear of the power they wield, and perhaps a secret personal ambition to one day lord over others. A more enlightened leadership style is the ruler who understands that the only legitimate power he or she has is in serving those who "follow." Besides that, there is no other power invested in the ruler. This is why Jesus washed the feet of his disciples. A true "servant leader" is charged to better others. That is his or her first and most important priority. Such leaders take it upon themselves to be of service, knowing that Albert Einstein was right when he said that "there is no greater satisfaction for a just and well-meaning person than the knowledge that he had devoted his best energies to the service of a good cause."

Each baby step in the right direction is still movement in the right direction. Great results can take time to measure. But the results will come. With effort and patience, change is more than possible—it's probable.

Let's give the last word to Henri Bergson, who wrote in his book *Final Remarks* that "action on the move creates its own route, creates to a very great extent the conditions under which it is to be fulfilled and thus baffles all calculations." Take action. And remember—a desired outcome awaits those who believe in their ability to effect change and who proceed with the bountiful force of soul intensity.

If You Win the Rat Race,
You're Still a Rat

Exactly who deserves the credit, no one is sure. Some say comedian Lily Tomlin coined the expression "If you win the rat race, you're still a rat" as part of a standup routine satirizing modern life. But in her book *A Short Guide to a Happy Life*, essayist Anna Quindlen says she learned the expression in a postcard from her father. Wherever it was born, one thing is for certain— the saying captures an archetypal truth of modern life.

Like rats in a maze, modern Americans often feel they are running to stand still. "If I had to describe my typical day," said a working mom recently, "it's a vicious cycle of rushing from place to place, with little time to catch my breath. Going to work, working, and getting home from work makes my life feel like I'm taking part in a marathon. I have no chance of winning."

"That's right," added the woman's husband. "After getting through the second shift of feeding, bathing, and tucking in our children, I sometimes spend the remainder of the evening at my desk, working through a mountain of bills, wondering how we ever got on this treadmill in the first place."

This is clearly a good question, definitely one worth asking. Maybe the place to start is at the beginning, examining how average people got so caught up in a life of acquisition.

The origin of the rat race, some analysts say, is our modern consumer culture. Predicated on the idea that a healthy economy is one that grows, a consumer culture thrives when people fuel economic growth with a steady stream of acquisitions. Whether they need those goods and services or not is another question entirely. In a culture of consumption, which thrives on an ever-growing bubble of expansion, marketers and advertisers make it their business to create desire for new, useless things and encourage dissatisfaction with "last year's model," whether it is still worthwhile or not.

Take an hour or two, if you've got the time, and tune in to watch the steady stream of advertisements. Using sophisticated tools of "subliminal persuasion," the marketers would like you to believe you will have more self-esteem, more love, and more power, among other attributes, if you put a down payment on that new car, new bracelet, or even take out a bank loan. Chrysler recently crafted a whole series of commercials around the slogan "Drive=Love," suggesting that the satisfaction one derives from a rich personal relationship might be also available by purchasing a car.

In his book *The Image: A Guide to Pseudo-Events in America*, Daniel Boorstin writes, "The successful advertiser is the master of a new art: the art of making things true by saying they are so. He is a devotee of the technique of self-fulfilling prophecy." As if this isn't bad enough, Boorstin adds, "The deeper problems connected with advertising come less from the unscrupulousness of our 'deceivers' than from our pleasure in being deceived, less from the desire to seduce than from the desire to be seduced."

Glued to their television sets, viewers have become entranced by what analyst Kalle Lasn calls a "media spectacle," combining mind-numbing programming with

 sales pitches. Advertisers and manufacturers have not only designed their commercials to hypnotize adults and children, they have set out to create a completely false worldview that undermines those who are underprivileged. "Studying the televised array of products and comforts available, seemingly, to everyone else, the poor become more dangerous," writes Barbara Ehrenreich in *Fear of Falling*. "There are no models, in the mainstream media, suggesting that anything less than middle-class affluence might be an honorable and dignified condition, nor is there any reason why corporate advertisers should promote such a subversive possibility."

While eradicating compassion, advertisements encourage a culture of inadequacy. Maybe that accounts for why so many Americans enter the rat race. All one needs to qualify is an appetite for waste and planned obsolescence. Why wear "last year's" clothing when you can be "in style" with the latest fashions? Why not feel good about yourself—you're such a putz as it is. All you need to do to enhance your sense of well-being is to get out your wallet. Once the image machine is in charge, consumers caught up in a cycle of acquisition may be willing to pay ghastly prices for unneeded things.

Underwriting this culture of inadequacy is a debt machine that encourages people to live above their heads —and feel good about it. "Congratulations," notes the credit card application, "for being awarded a Gold Card."

Anyone who watches television knows how easy it is to borrow, to get a new line of credit, to take out a second mortgage. Whether any of this is fiscally responsible is beside the point. Punishing interest rates are usually listed in the smallest possible print size for those who bother to look. Most don't bother until they become part of the growing ranks of people filing for bankruptcy.

Those who stay out of Chapter 11 still suffer mightily because they have mortgaged their future. Reaching above our heads is what has made the two-family income the norm in American life. While getting our exercise walking around the indoor mall, stuffing merchandise into our shopping bags, we tell ourselves that our "standard of living" has improved, but what about our "standard of life"? With stress levels at an all-time high, our precious health hangs in the balance. Not to mention our children, who are routinely farmed out to the growing industry of caregivers whose ranks have swelled in an effort to support two-career couples.

Is this a life we want to live? Do we want to rush around like tyrannical accumulators, being seduced by advertisers who tell us what we want to own—need to own—to be happy? Or do we want to return to an authentic life of simple abundance—one that acknowledges that the best things in life aren't things? Isn't it time to make a "declaration of enough"?

If you win the rat race, you're still a rat. One by one, people are starting to wake up to this profound truth. "It is pretty obvious that the debasement of the human mind caused by a constant flow of fraudulent advertising is no trivial thing," wrote Raymond Chandler. "There is more than one way to conquer a country." Though not necessarily more effective ways. In the fight to recover from the war of commercialization, each individual needs to take a stand against the forces of the marketing culture that tell us what we need to have. It is our unique responsibility to separate need and desire. And to take our power back.

Thankfully, there are positive signs that people are beginning to do exactly that. In Vancouver, British Columbia, the publishers of *Adbusters* magazine make it their monthly mission to expose the subliminal persuaders who encourage our children to smoke or emulate fashion models who are so painfully thin that they belong in treatment centers for anorexia. Kalle Lasn, the head of the Media Institute, which publishes *Adbusters,* is a self-styled freedom fighter against corporations who attempt to recruit and indoctrinate young consumers as early as possible.

Meanwhile, in another part of the world—Takoma Park, Maryland—the creative spirit is alive and well amid another vibrant band of idealists at the Center for a New America Dream, whose motto is "More fun, less stuff." The group's Web site and quarterly newsletter offer suggestions on how to enjoy life without getting mired down in debt, without going to the mall, and with more fulfillment than we thought possible. Cutting the commercial cord that has tied us to the purveyors of marketing and advertising, the center teaches its listeners how to use good old-fashioned creativity to strike a blow to the culture of commerce that has sponsored the rat race.

And let us not forget the inspiring voice of artists like José Saramago, the 1998 Nobel Laureate for Literature, who reflects on the corrosive effects of consumerism in his recent novel *The Cave.* A provocative work from the pen of a master, *The Cave* depicts a society dominated by a gigantic shopping mall called "The Center" that has become the vital hub of the community, housing hospitals and personal dwellings, as well as vending a wealth of products through a multivolume catalog thousands of pages long. "We would sell you everything you need," reads the Center's billboard, "but we would prefer you to need what we have to sell." "In José Saramago's nightmarish vision," *New York Times* critic Richard Eder writes, "the Western world is a commercial anaconda, devouring life and substituting itself in life's place."

Do we want to substitute our genuine experience of living for an increasingly ersatz reality? Do we want to run the rat race until we are so spiritually depleted that we drop down on the ground exhausted?"

Acknowledging the critics is only the first step in quitting the rat race. Even so, it's a start. Let's turn up the volume on people who speak out against the commercialization of everyday life and then give them our attention and support.

It's the Only Advice
You'll Ever Need

Imagine being selected to deliver a commencement message to graduating students all around the globe. Through the magic of closed circuit television—and with help from a battalion of translators—you can influence the next generation of leaders, doctors, lawyers, thinkers, scientists, and humanitarians before they leave school and go out into the world (or on to the next phase of their education). The assignment, should you choose to accept it, comes with just one hitch: You must convey your sentiments in twenty-five words or less.

Impossible? Don't give up so quickly. Throughout time, many of the most inspiring and powerful ideas have been offered in bite-sized nuggets of wisdom. If you don't believe it, consider the following list:

"Make new friends but keep the old, one is silver and the other's gold." —Anonymous

"Life is not linear. It ebbs and flows, like Yang and Yin. It's contradictions, the Unnamable, the Inexplicable. People don't plot anymore. They just flow." —Gail Godwin from *The Odd Woman*

"Don't Sweat the small stuff—and it's all small stuff." —Richard Carlson

"Trust life and it will teach you, in joy and sorrow, all you need to know." —James Baldwin

"No distance of space or lack of time can lessen the friendship of those who are thoroughly persuaded of each other's worth." —Robert Southey

"Love Your Neighbor as Yourself." —The Ten Commandments

"All life is an experiment. So what if you do fail and get

fairly rolled in the dirt once or twice?" —Ralph Waldo Emerson

"None of us can be as great as God, but any of us can be as good." —Mark Twain

"Do not take life too seriously—you will never get out of it alive." —Elbert Hubbard

"You're only here for a short visit. Don't hurry, don't worry, and be sure to smell the flowers along the way." —Walter Hagen, golfer

"Never cease to be convinced that life might be better —your own and other's; not a future life ... but this one of ours." —André Gide

"It is well to give when asked, but it is better to give unasked through understanding." —Kahlil Gibran

"Believe in something larger than yourself." —Barbara Bush

"I cannot and will not cut my conscience to fit this year's fashions." —Lillian Hellman

"Life is 10 percent what happens to me and 90 percent how I react to it." —Lou Holtz, football coach

"Bear with the faults and failings of others, for you, too, have many faults which others have to bear." —Thomas Kempis

"Life without commitment is not a life worth living. Just to live is holy." —Abraham Joshua Heschel

"Govern thy Life and Thought as if the whole World were to see the one and read the other." —Thomas Fuller

"There are three ingredients to a good life: Learning, earning and yearning." —Christopher Morley

"There is an idea abroad among moral people that they should make their neighbors good. One person I have to make good—myself." —Robert Louis Stevenson

"The law of our life can be summed up in the axiom: Be What You Are." —Thomas Merton

"One must never, for whatever reason, turn his back on life." —Eleanor Roosevelt

OK, now that you've seen what others have to offer, it's your turn. As you add your ideas to these rich and diverse offerings, bear in mind one last piece of advice. It is purely and simply the idea that:

THE BEST THINGS IN LIFE AREN'T THINGS

For what it's worth, I know that these seven simple words are full of truth. Since taking them to heart, my own life has become richer and more meaningful. But don't take my word for it—try it out; tell your friends; offer this sentiment to people you care about, as well as to the graduates of tomorrow who will shape our world. And see if you don't eventually come to discover that it's the only advice you'll ever really need.

A Directory of the Best Things That Aren't Things

If you were asked to create a directory of the best things in life—*the things that aren't things*—what would you include? You are welcome to list anything that doesn't cost money. No designer jeans or Italian sunglasses. No sports cars or diamond rings. You get the idea. In order to help get your creative juices flowing, I've taken the initiative to set down some thoughts. Here are more than two hundred possible entries that draw upon virtues, principles, experiences, emotions, and the awe-inspiring beauty of nature—the intangibles that create quality of life.

Being forgiven

The courage of our convictions

Sympathetic words during tough times

A sense of decency

Achieving a win-win situation

Thinking outside the box

Encountering raw talent

Lunching with an old friend

Viewing the fresh morning dew on the grass

Experiencing a cleansing rain

The smell of fresh baked bread

Simples acts of kindness and humility

Solving a problem with a creative solution

Walking on the beach at sunset

Counting a baby's toes

Snuggling together on a cold night before a
    crackling fire

Listening to the pure voices of a children's choir

Belly laughing at a funny movie or a good joke

Reaching your destination

Coming home

Saying the words "I do"

Hearing the whisper of the wind

Gathering with family at Thanksgiving

Holding a family reunion

Relaxing on vacation

Taking a nap

Waking up refreshed

Feeling inspired by art, poetry, or music

Feeling at one with nature

Celebrating a holiday with close friends and family

Going on summer vacation

Being inspired by poetry

The feel of grass tickling your toes

The wailing of a newborn baby

Enjoying a good book

Watching a good movie

Having a good cry that washes away the sorrow
Admiring a painting
Getting lost in a piece of music
Singing in the shower
Jack Frost nipping at your nose
Drinking hot cocoa in the depths of winter
Hearing the roar of the ocean
Lying down in the splendor of the grass
Smelling fresh flowers in bloom
Seeing a splash of color in the sky at sunset
Acknowledging the rich mosaic of life
Feeling needed
Being let off the hook
Finding a calm port in a tumultuous storm
Hearing the peal of church bells pierce
    the stillness of the day
Noticing the changing autumn colors
Crunching leaves under your feet
Leaf peeping during fall foliage season

Being licked by an affectionate puppy
Noticing a newborn animal's tail wagging
Holding a baby kitten, monkey, or bird
Smelling morning coffee
Hearing the chatter of a babbling brook
Hearing someone ask, "Can I help?"
Two hearts beating as one
Experiencing peace of mind
Shedding tears of joy
Soaking up the warm rays of the sun
Catching raindrops with your tongue
Making snow angels
Cuddling with someone you love on a stormy night
Knowing someone really cares
Getting a taste of puppy love
The moment you knew you found your soul mate
Seeing sunlight stream into your room
Spotting a firefly on a summer night
Taking a coffee break

A moment of stillness in a boat on a lake

Having free time

Being true to your word

Keeping a solemn vow

Babies' first words

The sound of silence

The still of the night

Walking down a country road

Dancing until dawn

Holding hands

Running into an old friend

Reliving a cherished memory

Being a good loser

Making the cut

Hearing the sound of the key in the lock so you can
    go to sleep after waiting up

Seeing the difference you've made in someone's life

Reminiscing about the good old times

Getting a clean bill of health

Hearing a grandchild say, "I love you, Papa"
Feeding the hungry
Clothing the naked
Tending the sick
Showing mercy
Taking the high road
Being magnanimous toward someone who is difficult
Coming up for air after a busy period
Going the extra mile
Rescuing a stray
Being true to yourself
Standing on principle
Doing the right thing
Scoring the winning run
Skipping stones on the water
Choosing to remain faithful
Growing old gracefully
Getting to know yourself and liking who you are
Allowing yourself to be imperfect

Reading a love letter

Writing a love letter

Finding old photos and treasured memories in the attic

Sharing a secret with a friend

Forgiving, not just forgetting

Climbing into a bed with clean sheets

Speaking the truth

Being of service

Following a good leader

Collaborating with like-minded people

Pursuing a worthy goal

Taking your time

Expressing the creative urge

Thinking on your feet

Achieving a balanced life

Having all the ingredients

Offering a measured response in a difficult situation

Summoning the strength to surmount adversity

Having what it takes

Capturing a precious moment on film

Knowing when to say no

Turning on the radio and hearing "our song"

Getting a lump in your throat at a good movie

Receiving a little tea and sympathy when you
    most need it

Standing up for what's right—even if you stand alone

Traveling to the beat of a different drum—and feeling
    triumphant because of it

Sleeping outside, under the stars

Taking a walk on the wild side

Basking in the afterglow of a good time

Kissing a child to make his or her boo-boo feel better

Eating home-grown foods from your own garden

Finishing a race you've trained to run for charity

Attaining a sense of completion

Bringing something that is nearly dead back to life

Achieving a personal best

Stealing beauty

Holding fast to a potent sense of idealism

Achieving a spiritual high

Participating in an enriching experience

Knowing that you have formed a meaningful
    relationship

Finally getting through to someone who is stubborn

Gathering in a community of like-minded individuals

Achieving serenity

Being inspired to be idealistic

Reuniting with old friends

Exchanging tokens of affection with someone
    you admire

Reveling in the presence of a beloved companion

A spirit of generosity

A humble bearing

A heart of caring

A compassionate nature

A refreshing afternoon nap

A sleeping baby

Arriving at your destination
Holding hands with a kindred spirit
Having a brainstorm that provides a solution
Being invited for a home-cooked meal
Collecting seashells
Making peace with your parents
Looking at a situation with fresh eyes
Getting the most out of an experience
Not losing any sleep over something that could
    be troubling
Putting things into perspective
Knowing that the darkest hour is just before the dawn
Finding inspiration in an unlikely place
Going easy on someone when your inclination is to
    come down hard
Nurturing a gift
Being sensitive to someone's feelings
Hearing the call of the wild
Noticing first tracks in the freshly fallen snow

Coming home for the holidays

Finishing up a difficult task

Holding fast to a vision

Discovering the key that unlocks your troubles

Flirting with danger but not giving in

Practicing self-discipline

Not taking advantage

Following a code of honor

Not jumping to false conclusions

Not bearing false witness

Finding some breathing space

Remembering that life is what you make it

Finding the courage to change

Hitting one out of the park

Taking a mental health day

Going on a retreat

Finding the perfect gift for someone you love

Coming out on top

Achieving a complete recovery

Making amends

Getting straight A's

Healing an old wound

Daydreaming about the good old days

Having a clean slate

Making real progress

Catching a big one

Not having a care in the world

Taking a load off your mind

Doing your best

Being a good example

Saying strong things gently, and gentle
    things strongly

Meting out justice

Speaking the truth in love and loving
    the truth in each

Having a positive frame of mind

Getting to yes

Achieving détente

Reaching a happy medium
Finding a healthy compromise
Knowing that someone special really cares about you
Remembering the good times, honoring the bad
Letting go of fear

Now It's Your Turn

In the space provided below, tell us what you consider the best things in your life. Make sure to share them with someone you love.

Sharing Wisdom with Those You Love

If you had to pass on a single piece of advice to the people you love to help guide their lives, what would it be? Use the space below to impart your special observations and wisdom.

Resources

Affluenza, the videotape, shown on PBS, and marketed through Bull Frog Films

Bartlett's Book of Familiar Quotations

Quotationary by Leonard Roy Frank (Inspiring and comprehensive, this book is more than a reference work. Its author must be commended for his outstanding job of pulling together some of the most provocative ideas of all time into one handy volume that makes for great reading.)

For information on the Voluntary Simplicity Movement, you can contact: Seeds of Simplicity, P.O. CBox 9955, Glendale, CA 91226, 818-247-4332, www.seedsof-simplicity.org

For information about the "Best Things" bumper sticker, log on to www.progressivecatalog.com

And for information about the Center for a New American Dream, you can contact them at: The Center for a New American Dream, 6930 Carroll Ave., Suite 900, Takoma Park, MD 20912, 301-891-3683, www.newdream.org. The Center's president, Betsy Taylor, is the author of an inspiring parenting book, *What Kids Really Want That Money Can't Buy.*

Acknowledgments

Allowing that all the errors in this book are mine alone, I would like to thank the many people who have contributed to my life and to my work. To each who has given generously and with heart, I am profoundly grateful.

Starting with the people at Beacon Press who took a chance on this project. First thanks go to Gayatri Patnaik, who was there in the beginning with belief and enthusiasm. How stunning that your integrity and spirit are matched by all of your colleagues: Kerri Bowen, Pam MacColl, Tom Hallock, David Coen, Helene Atwan, P. J. Tierney, and Katie O'Neil, who gave me support and encouragement for which I will forever be grateful.

Thanks also to Tim Maher, who did a masterful copy-editing job.

To the people at another publishing company—Warner Books—who first urged me on my path in book publishing. Larry Kirshbaum, I will never forget your casual remark uttered over breakfast to "come work for us" when I was still at *Publishers Weekly* and restless for new direction. You truly changed my life by teaching me how to go for it. My deepest thanks go as well to Jamie Raab, my cherished friend, and Rick Horgan, my unparalleled colleague, who urged me to "write something" and find a voice, and to Liv Blumer, also formerly of Warner, who has a degree in straight talk and always urges me to stay in the center of what needs to be done, should be done.

To my many supportive friends—Joyce Waldon, Douglas Danoff, David Black, Joy Tutela, Michelle Shinseki, Susan Raihofer, Linda Watson, Star Gibbs, Carla Tanzi, Maggie Hamilton, Lynn Hinton, Marcy

Goot, and Joyce Vedral—each of you has made me know the meaning of community. And to Albert, the one and only "Prince of Clear," who was always there to show me encouragement and sensitivity when I needed nothing but. To Kathryn Adams Shapiro—I could not have gotten through it without you and the gift of healing you have in your hands and heart. And to Doris Wilde Helmering, Michael Colberg, Gerry Celente, and Lois Harding, each of you were there, playing a role that I shall never forget.

To the memory of Bill Biggart and Larry Virgilio, who died at the Towers but whose spirit lives on in each life they touched. We remember. We will never forget.

And to the "professor," Dr. Leslie Erdos. Though you never got the recognition you deserved for your philosophical theories, you uniquely shaped my worldview. I hope I am a worthy student of the lessons you taught me.

To my mother, father, and sisters, Anna, Paul, Paula,

Donna, and especially Ellen, who reminded me of "the best things" when I forgot. Thanks you all for demonstrating what it means to care every day in every way and for doing the best you can. None should expect more.

And to my own children, Jenny and Colin, who each day, without knowing, teach me standards of decency and integrity, of optimism and courage, and who truly hold the future of the world in their hands. You are my inspiration and my gift. You make each minute of each day a breathtaking adventure. God has made no equal to what you provide me.

And finally, to Kenny. Sharing a life with you would be a treasure enough. But you have taught me about the meaning of love, what true caring is all about. For this great lesson there are no words. Only the steady beating of my heart.